BUDDHA
LAUGHING

a tricycle book of cartoons

BUDDHA

LAUGHING

BELL TOWER / New York

Published by Bell Tower, New York, New York.
Member of the Crown Publishing Group.

Random House, Inc. New York, Toronto, London, Sydney, Auckland
www.randomhouse.com

Bell Tower and colophon are registered trademarks of Random House, Inc.

Printed in the United States of America

DESIGN BY KAREN MINSTER

Library of Congress Cataloging-in-Publication Data
Buddha laughing : A Tricycle book of cartoons—1st ed.
Includes index.
1.Buddhism—Caricatures and cartoons.
I. Tricycle (New York, N.Y.).
BQ4030.B84   1999
294.3'02'07—dc21   98-46340

ISBN 0-609-80409-X

10   9   8   7   6

ACKNOWLEDGMENTS

These cartoons have been graciously contributed to *Tricycle: The Buddhist Review* for this volume. Over the years, many of them have appeared in the magazine, adding to a serious subject touches of levity that have been sorely needed. Yet in collection, their intelligence and wisdom reveal a salutary and unique tributary of the American Dharma stream.

All proceeds of this book go to The Buddhist Ray, a not-for-profit educational organization that publishes the magazine. *Tricycle* wishes to thank each of the artists for their work and wit, and for their support; as well, deserving of special mention are Katharine Shields, Jayanti Tamm, and Neal Crosbie.

BUDDHA
LAUGHING

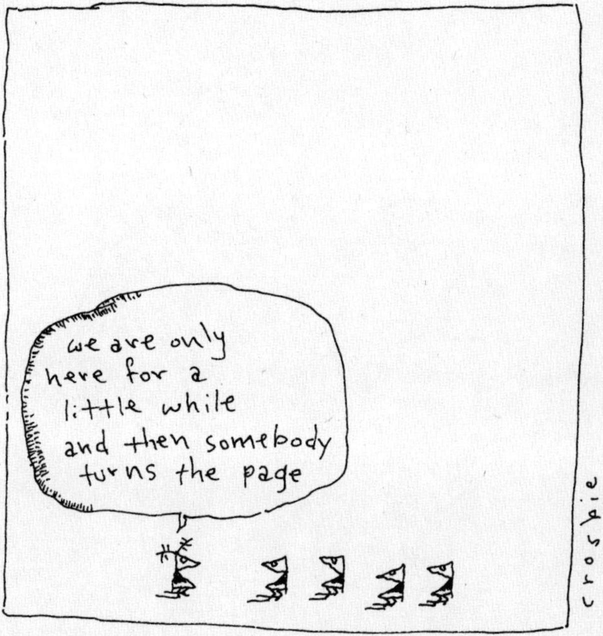
we are only here for a little while and then somebody turns the page
crosbie

"*This man says you're the reincarnation of Jimmy Stewart, and you belong in L.A.*"

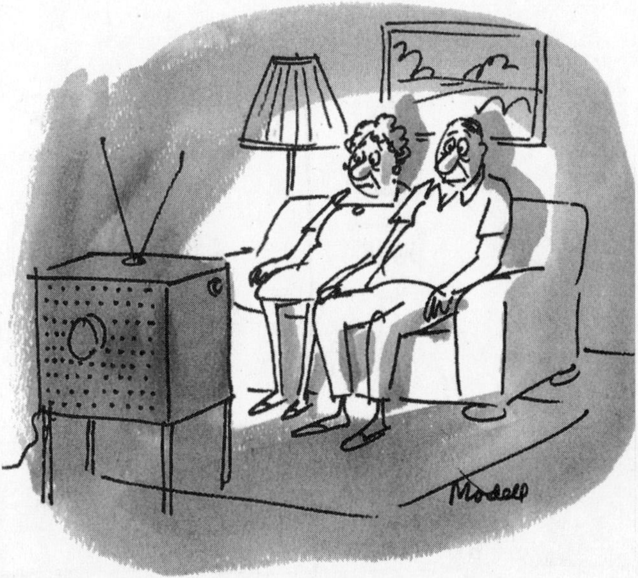
Modell

"It's ten o'clock. Do you know where your mind is?"

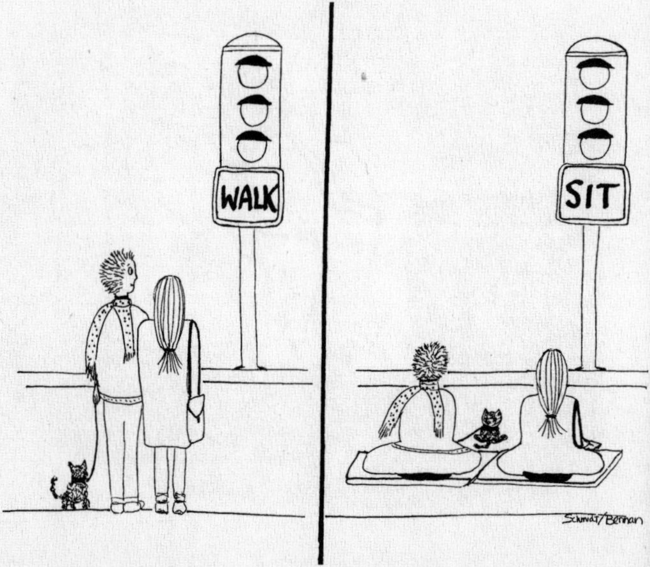
WALK
SIT
Schmidt/Berman

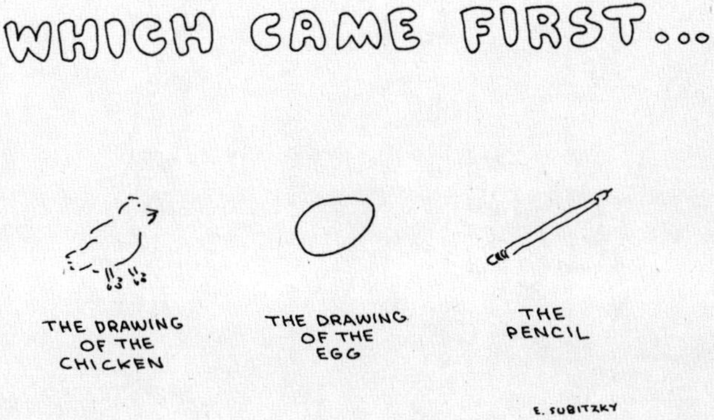
WHICH CAME FIRST...
THE DRAWING OF THE CHICKEN
THE DRAWING OF THE EGG
THE PENCIL
E. SUBITZKY

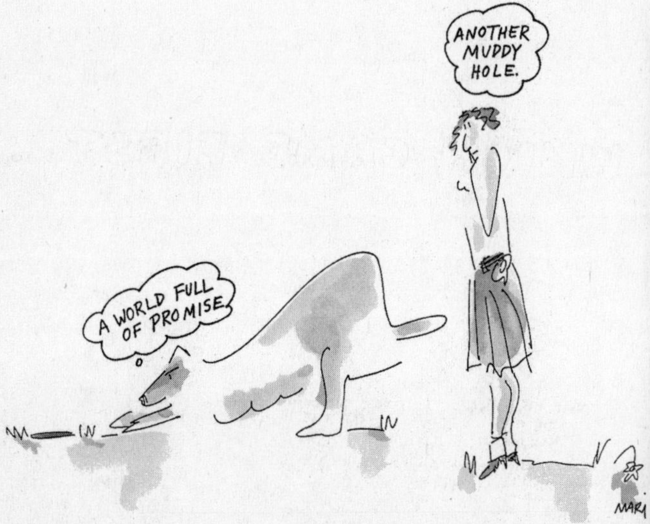
ANOTHER MUDDY HOLE.
A WORLD FULL OF PROMISE

From holes to wholeness.

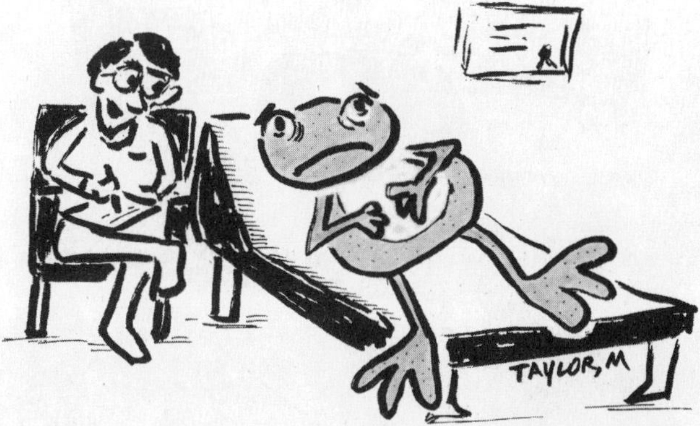
TAYLOR, M

"When did you first have the notion that poets were writing haiku about you?"

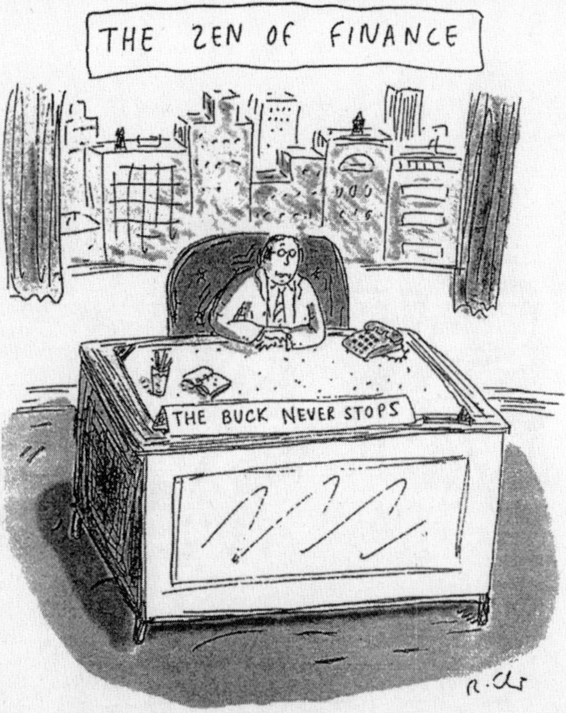
THE ZEN OF FINANCE
THE BUCK NEVER STOPS

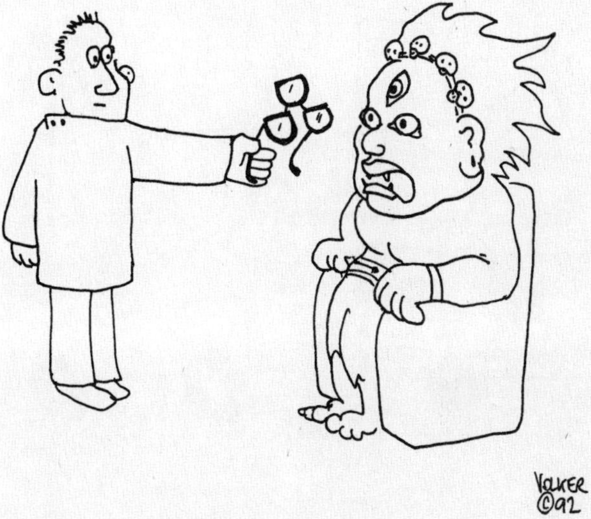
VOLKER
©92

Mahakala at the eye doctor.

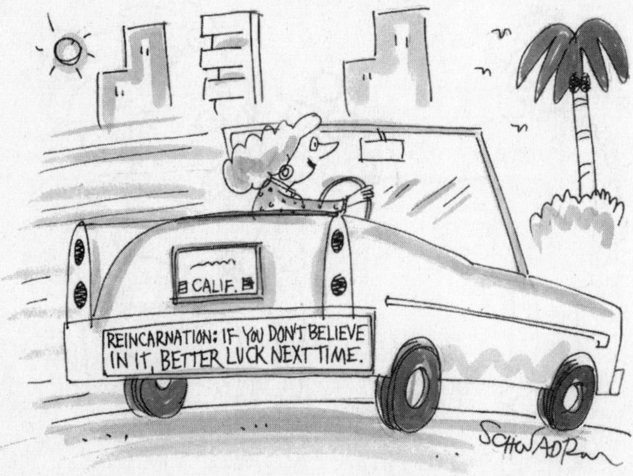
CALIF.
REINCARNATION: IF YOU DON'T BELIEVE IN IT, BETTER LUCK NEXT TIME.
SCHWADRON

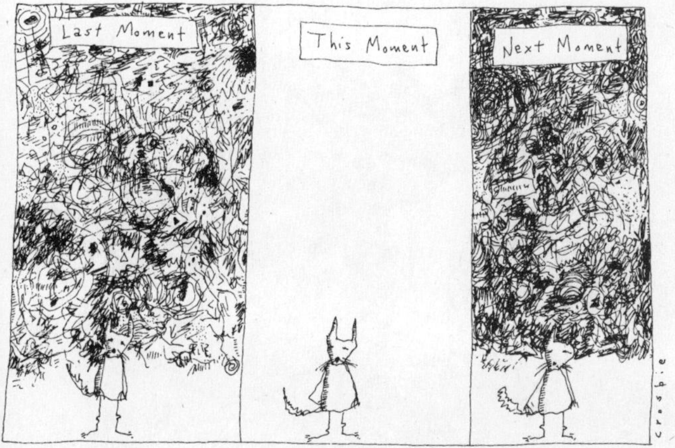
Last Moment
This Moment
Next Moment
crosbie

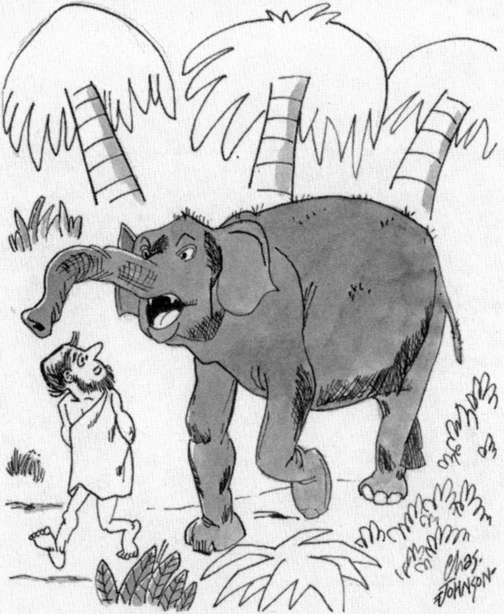
Chas. Johnson

"As your mother, I knew what was best for you in my last life, Herman, and I still know. . . ."

DR. OF
PSYCHIATRY
E. SUBITZKY

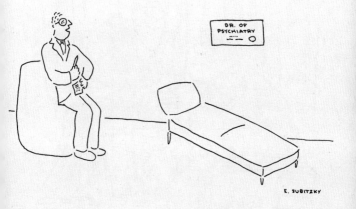

"So, Mr. Smithers, when did you first discover that your sense of self was just an illusion?"

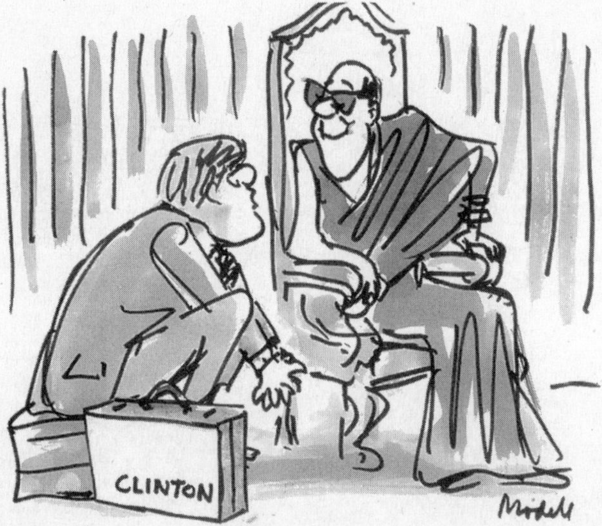
CLINTON
Modell

"*Your Holiness, are you absolutely*
sure *there is no oil in Tibet?*"

PERSONALS

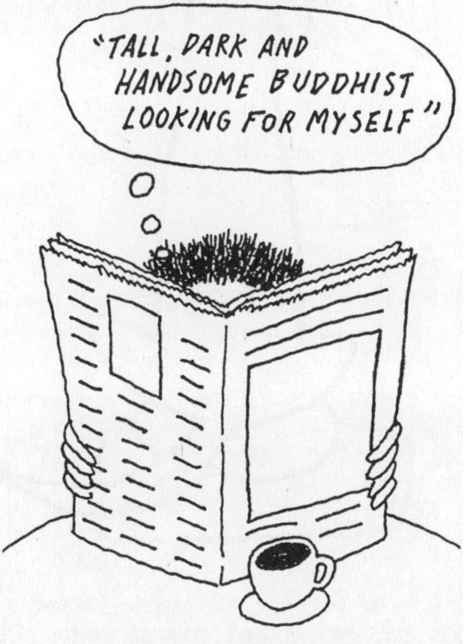
"TALL, DARK AND HANDSOME BUDDHIST LOOKING FOR MYSELF"

"... no eyes, no ears, no nose, no tail ..."

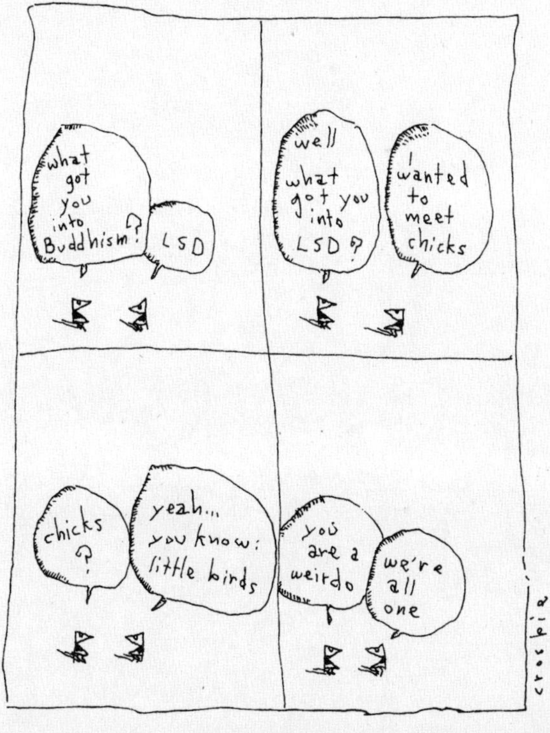
what got you into Buddhism?
LSD
well what got you into LSD?
I wanted to meet chicks
chicks?
yeah... you know: little birds
you are a weirdo
we're all one
crockett

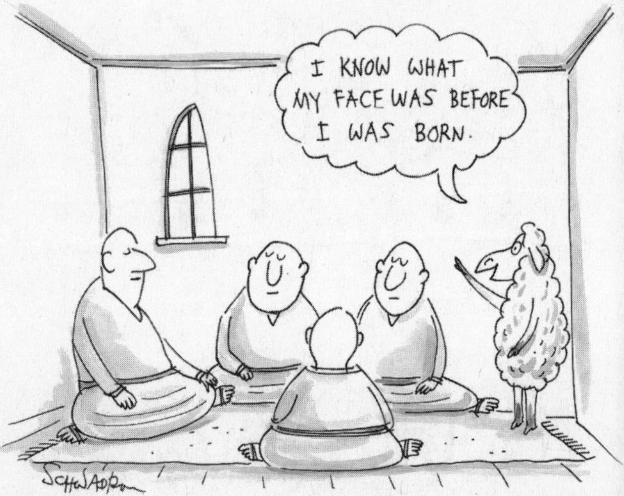
I KNOW WHAT MY FACE WAS BEFORE I WAS BORN.
SCHWADRON

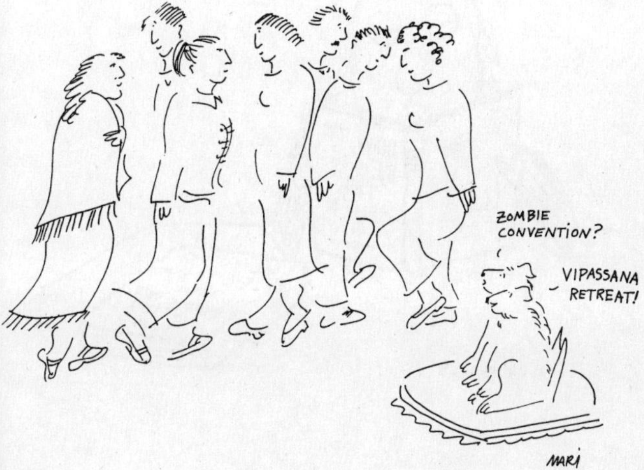
ZOMBIE CONVENTION?
VIPASSANA RETREAT!
MARI

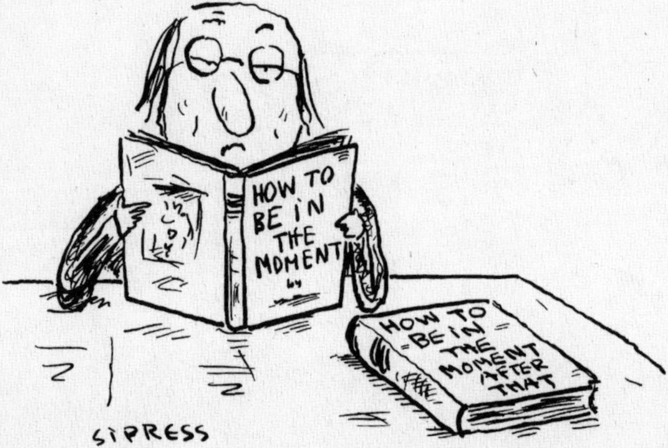
HOW TO
BE IN
THE
MOMENT
HOW TO
BE IN
THE
MOMENT
AFTER
THAT
SIPRESS

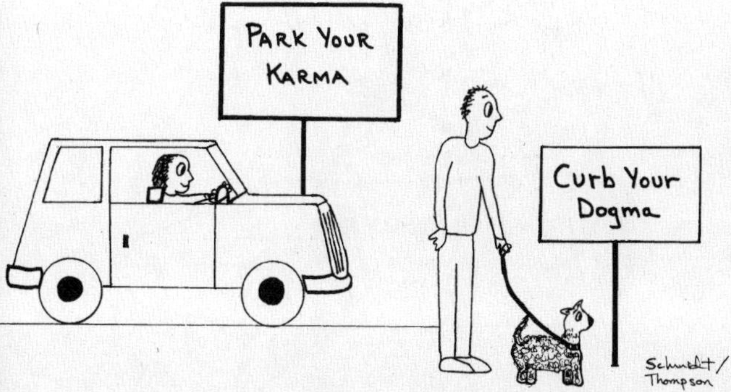
PARK YOUR KARMA
Curb Your Dogma
Schmidt/ Thompson

ZEN VACUUM CLEANER

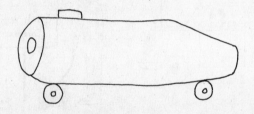

(NO ATTACHMENTS)

E. SUBITZKY

TODAY'S SPECIAL: $2.00
PAINFUL YOGA POSTURES
THAT YOU CAN EAT!

TAYLOR, M

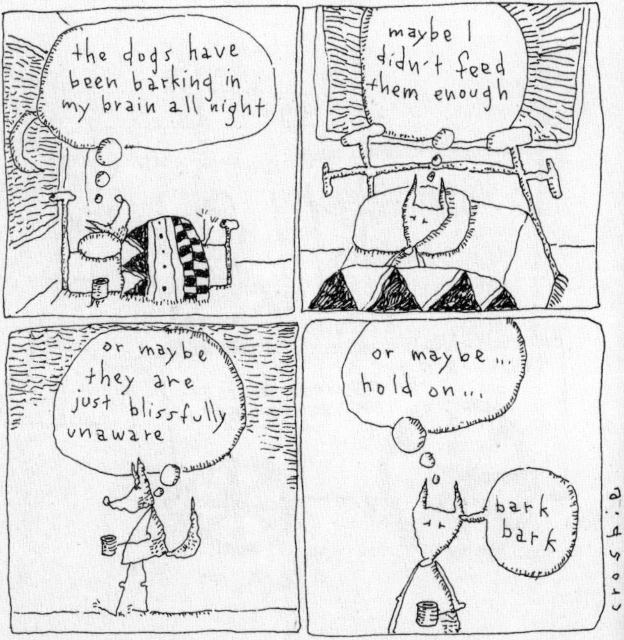
the dogs have been barking in my brain all night
maybe I didn't feed them enough
or maybe they are just blissfully unaware
or maybe... hold on...
bark bark
crosbie

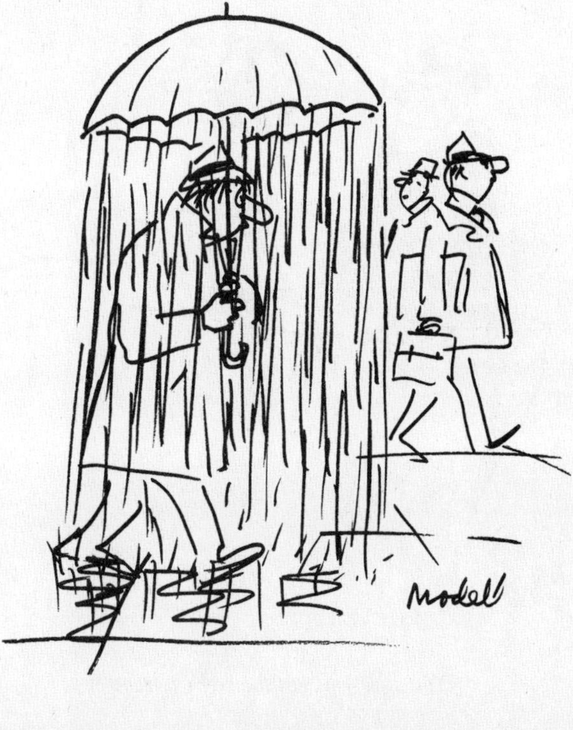
Model

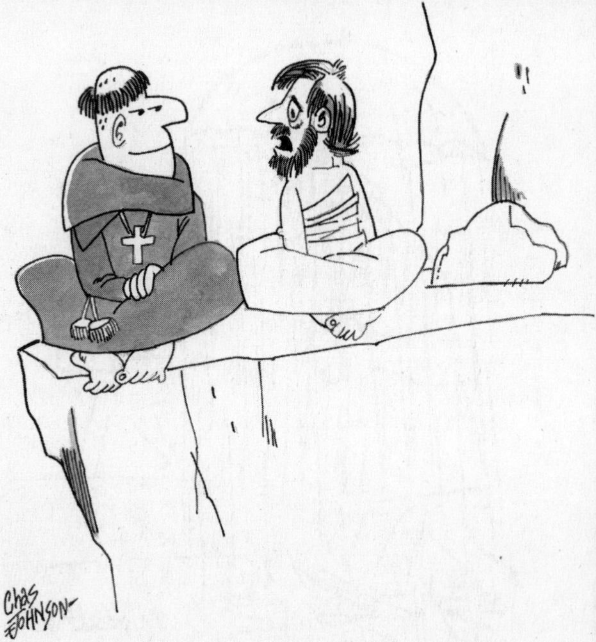
Chas Johnson

"You sure you got the right retreat?"

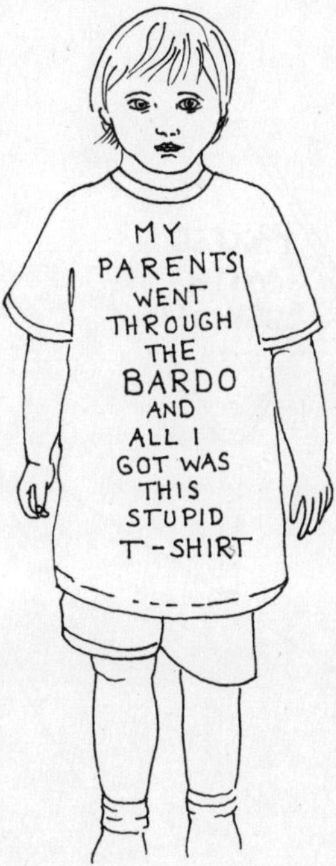
MY
PARENTS
WENT
THROUGH
THE
BARDO
AND
ALL I
GOT WAS
THIS
STUPID
T-SHIRT

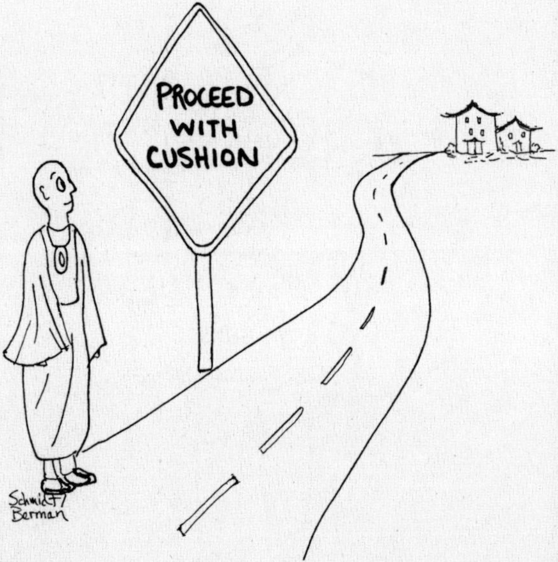
PROCEED
WITH
CUSHION
Schmidt/
Berman

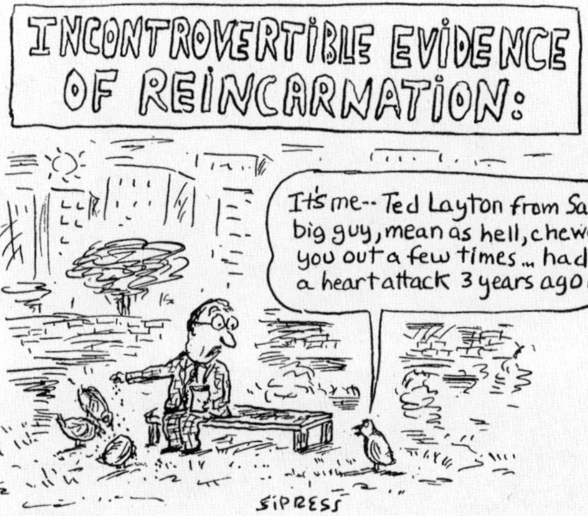
INCONTROVERTIBLE EVIDENCE OF REINCARNATION:
It's me-- Ted Layton from Sales... big guy, mean as hell, chewed you out a few times... had a heart attack 3 years ago...
SIPRESS

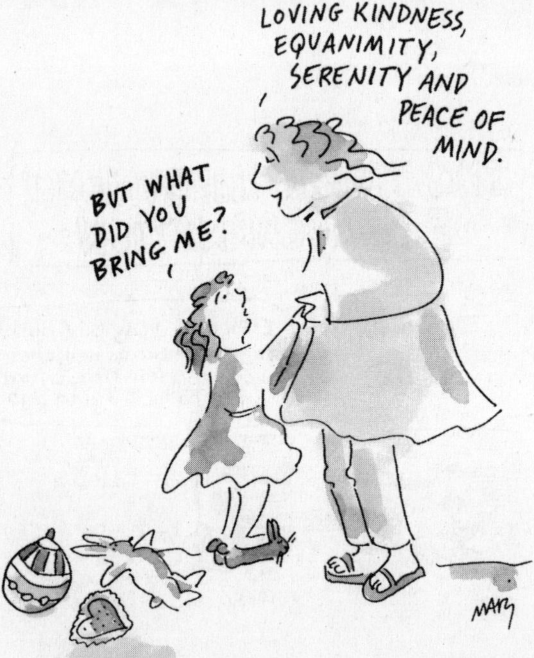
LOVING KINDNESS, EQUANIMITY, SERENITY AND PEACE OF MIND.
BUT WHAT DID YOU BRING ME?
MARY

When Mommy gets home from her metta retreat.

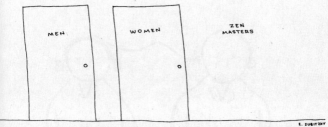

MEN · WOMEN · ZEN MASTERS

E. SUBITZKY

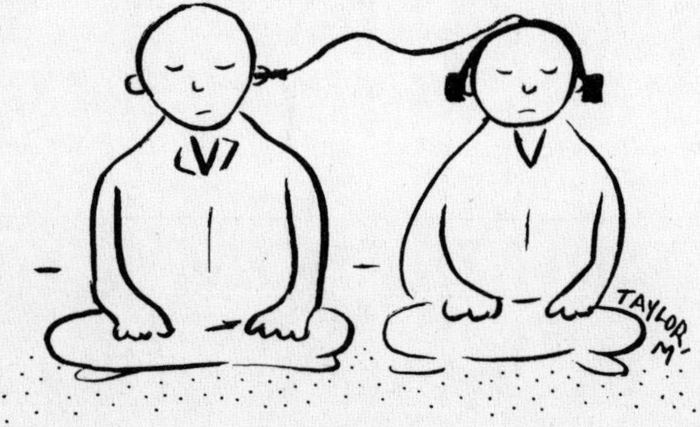
TAYLOR
M'

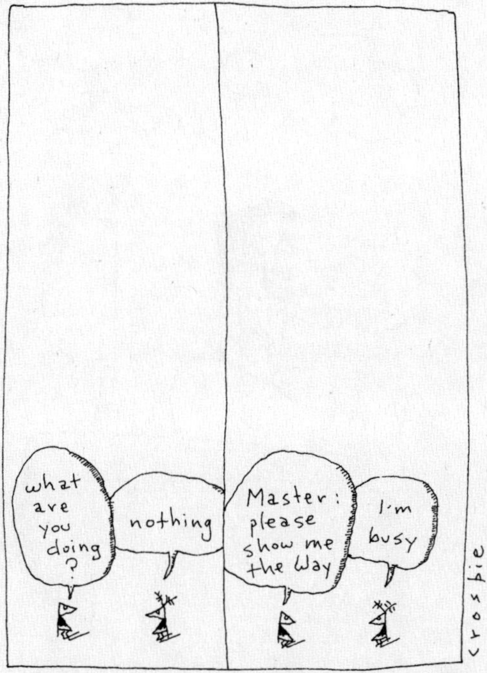
what are you doing?
nothing
Master: please show me the Way
I'm busy
crosbie

"Om . . . om . . . om . . . om . . . om . . . om . . ."

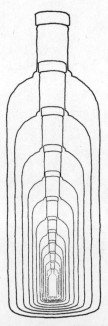

ABSOLUT REINCARNATION.

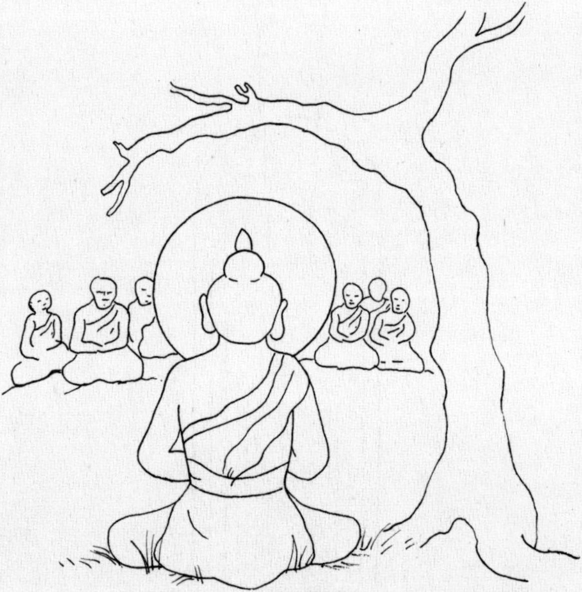

"O monks! How do you feel about starting a men's group?"

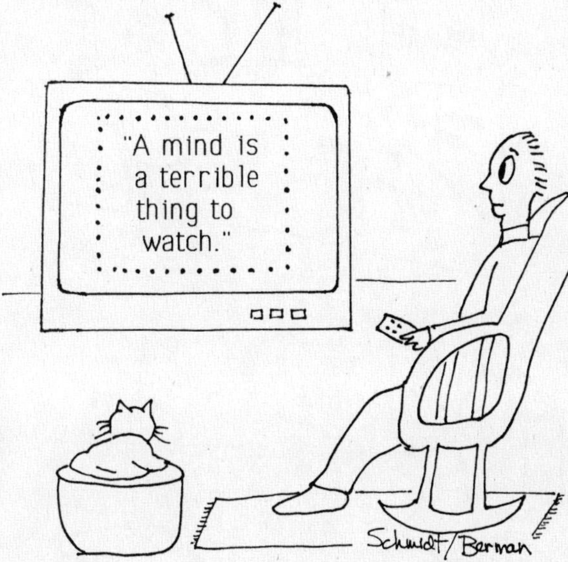
"A mind is a terrible thing to watch."
Schmidt/Berman

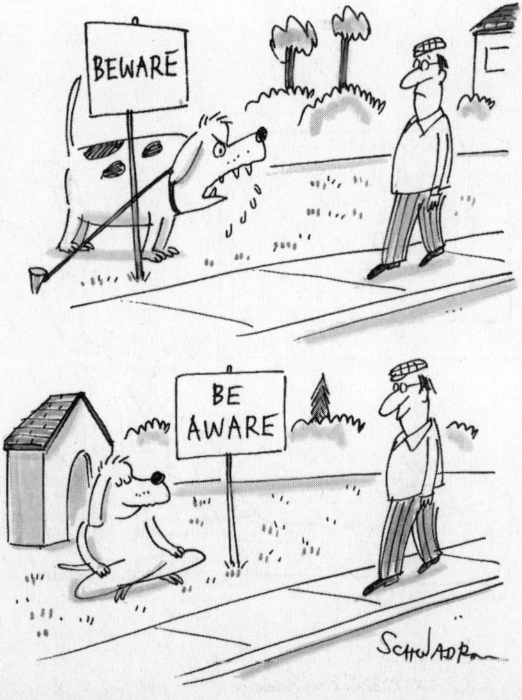
BEWARE
BE AWARE
SCHWADRON

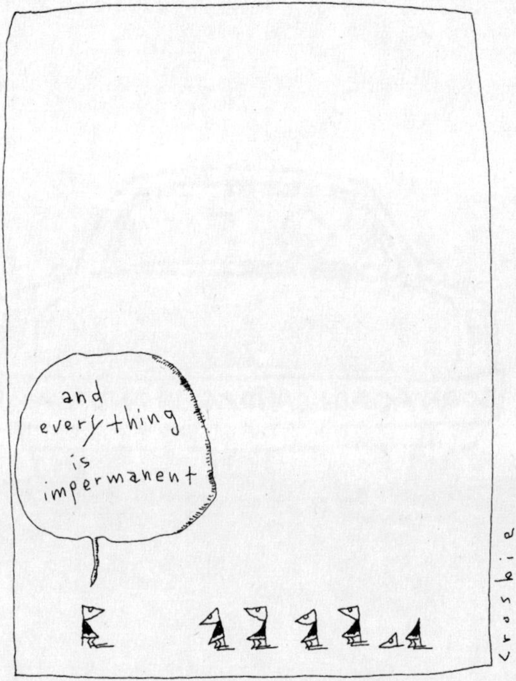
and everything is impermanent
Crosbie

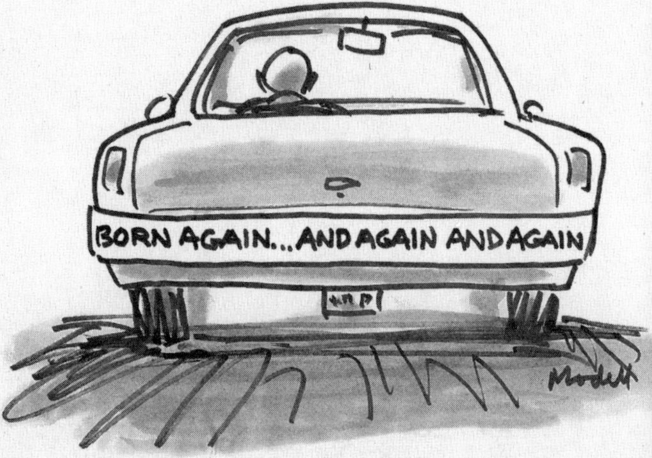
BORN AGAIN...AND AGAIN AND AGAIN

DETERMINED MEDITATOR

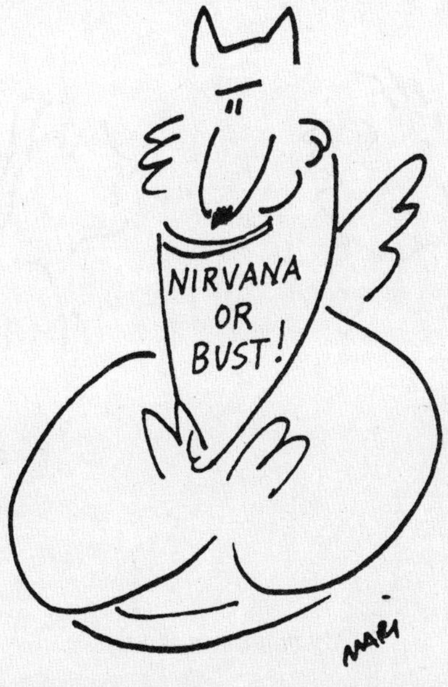
NIRVANA
OR
BUST!
MARI

E. SUBITZKY

"My mantra or yours?"

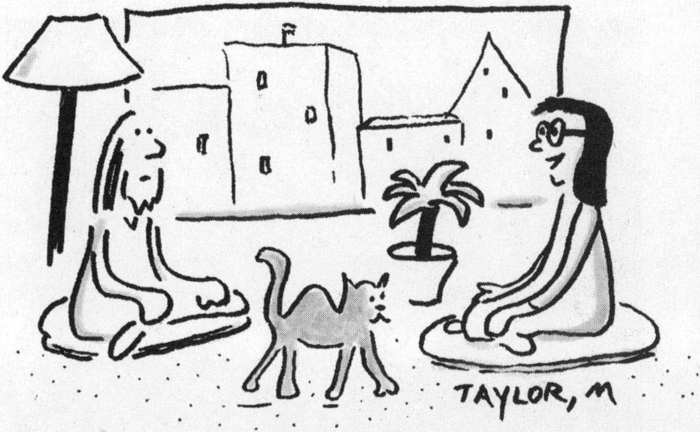
TAYLOR, M

"Fluffy's the ninth reincarnation of herself."

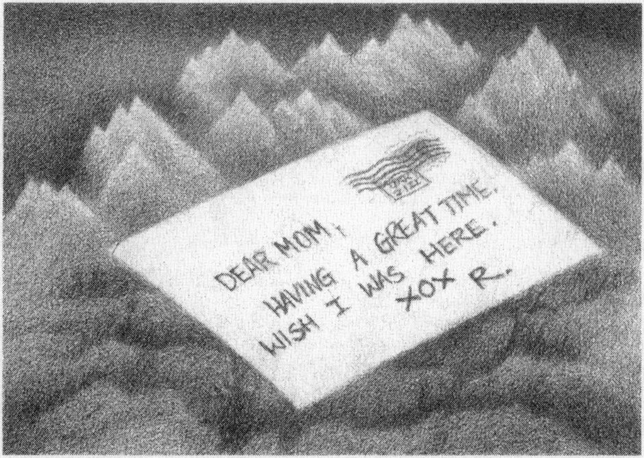
DEAR MOM,
HAVING A GREAT TIME.
WISH I WAS HERE.
XOX R.

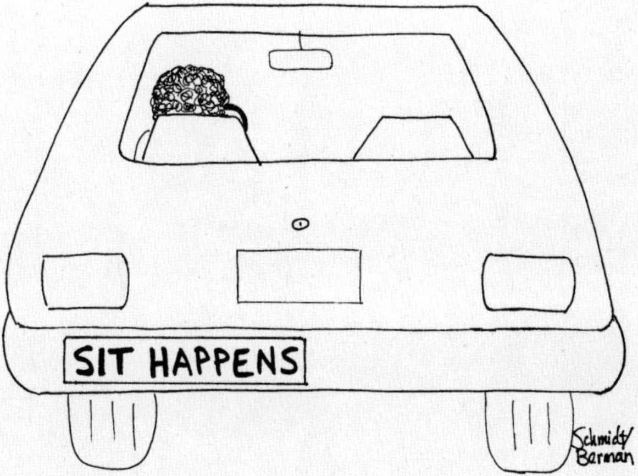
SIT HAPPENS
Schmidt/
Berman

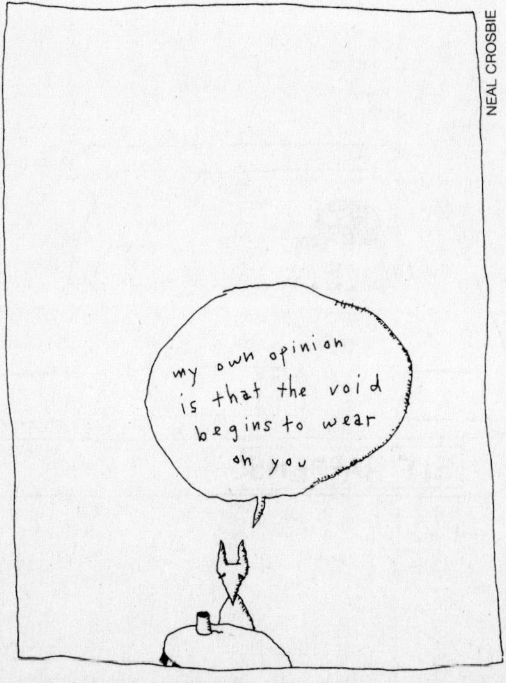
my own opinion is that the void begins to wear on you

NEAL CROSBIE

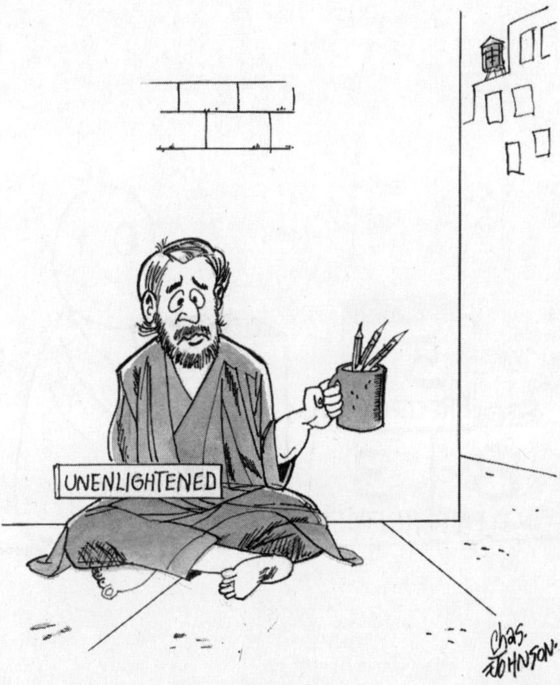
UNENLIGHTENED
Chas. Johnson.

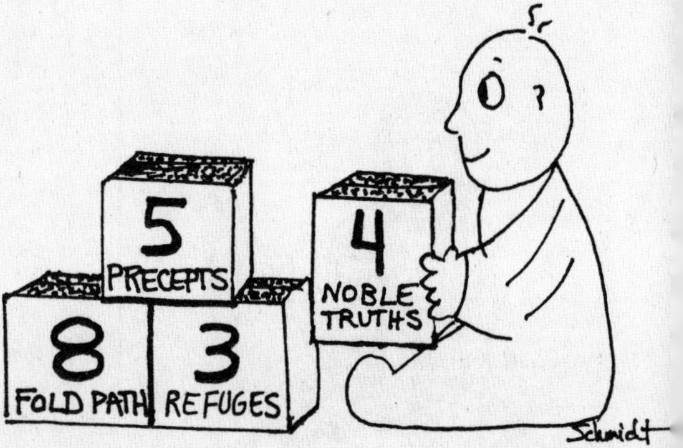
5
PRECEPTS
4
NOBLE
TRUTHS
8
FOLD PATH
3
REFUGES
Schmidt

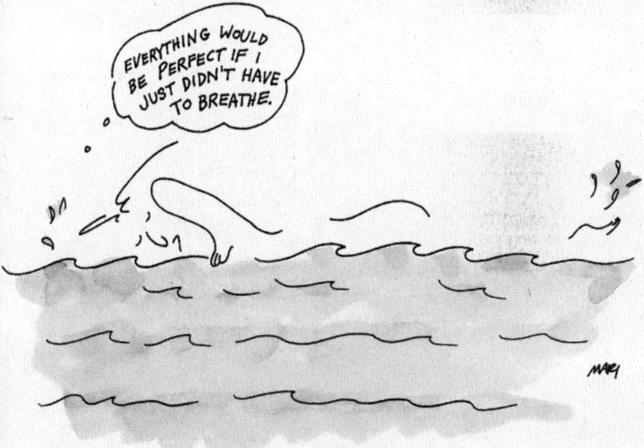
EVERYTHING WOULD BE PERFECT IF I JUST DIDN'T HAVE TO BREATHE.

Insights of a meditating swimmer.

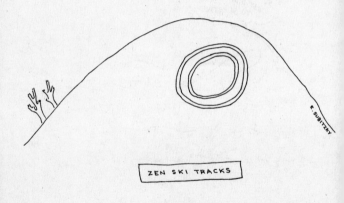

E. SUBITZKY

ZEN SKI TRACKS

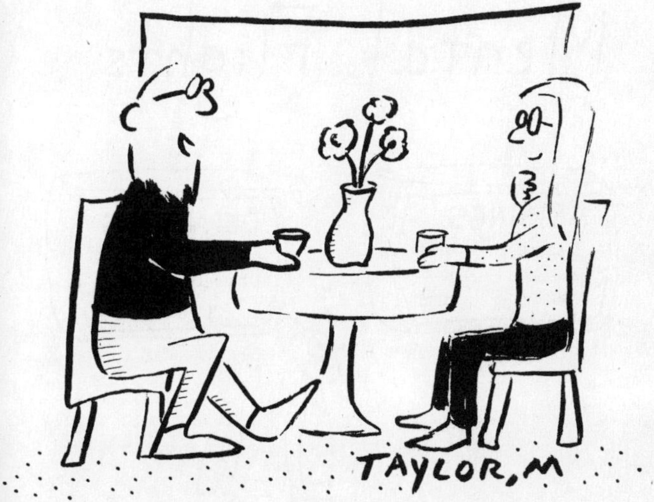
TAYLOR, M

"I'm a nonsmoker and a reformed carnivore."

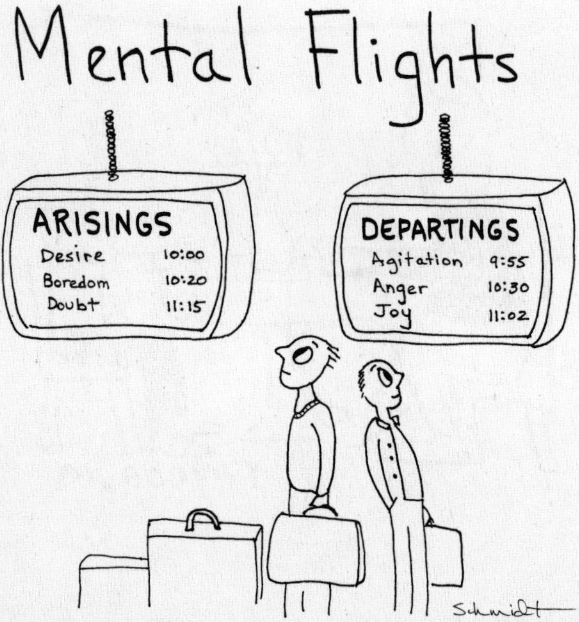
Mental Flights
ARISINGS
Desire 10:00
Boredom 10:20
Doubt 11:15
DEPARTINGS
Agitation 9:55
Anger 10:30
Joy 11:02
Schmidt

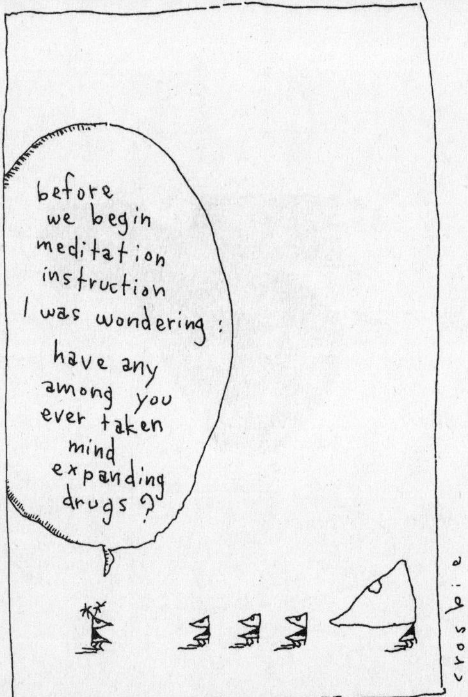
before we begin meditation instruction I was wondering: have any among you ever taken mind expanding drugs?
crosbie

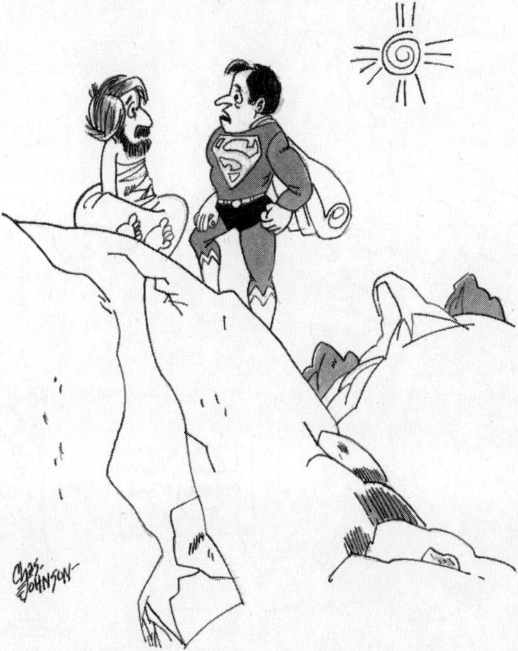
CHAS. JOHNSON

"How can I conquer my ego?"

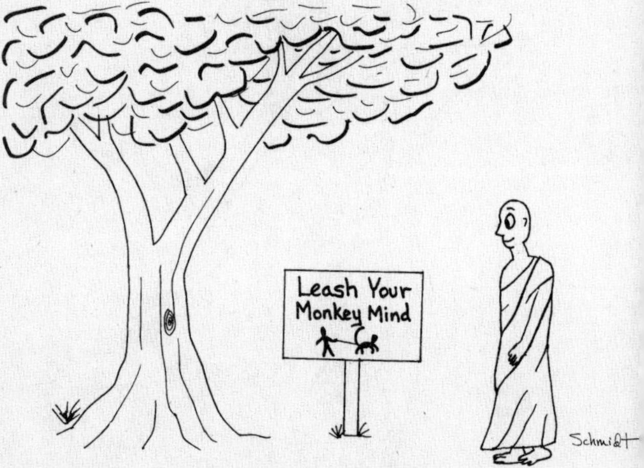
Leash Your
Monkey Mind
Schmidt

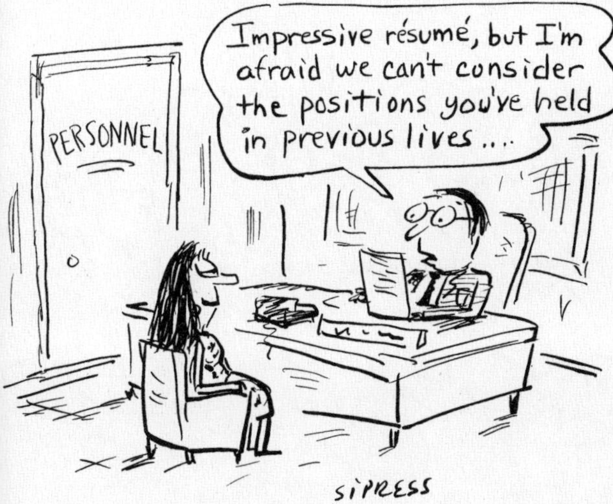
Impressive résumé, but I'm afraid we can't consider the positions you've held in previous lives . . .
PERSONNEL
SIPRESS

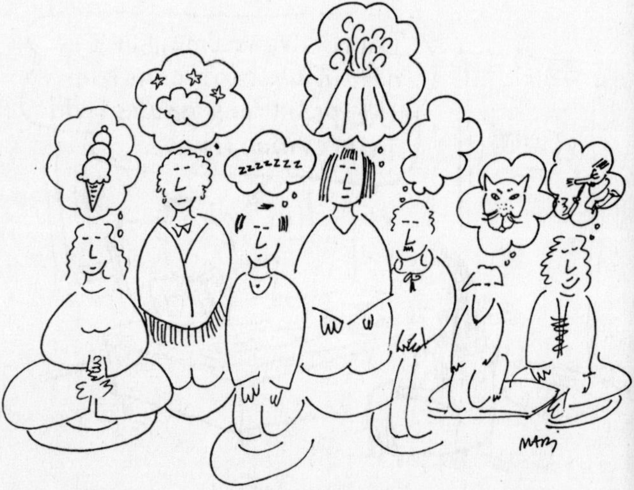
zzzzzzz

Awareness and nonawareness of the arising of the hindrances.

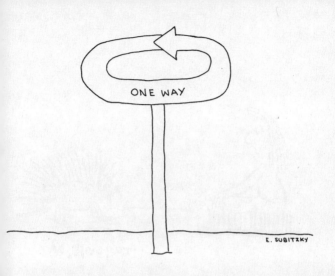

ONE WAY

E. SUBITZKY

ZEN STREET SIGN

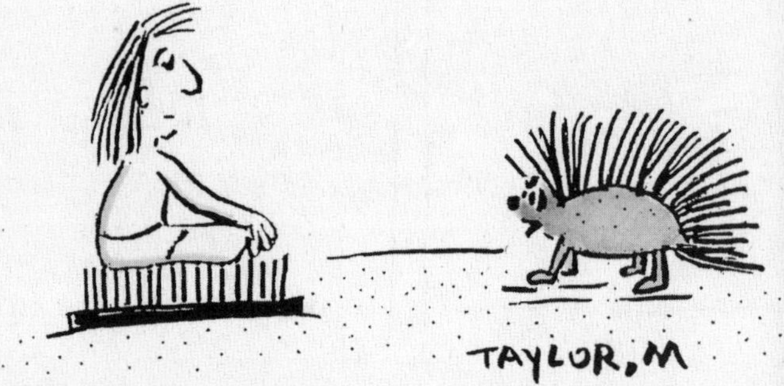
TAYLOR, M

"Wake up, young man—you're ruining your pelt."

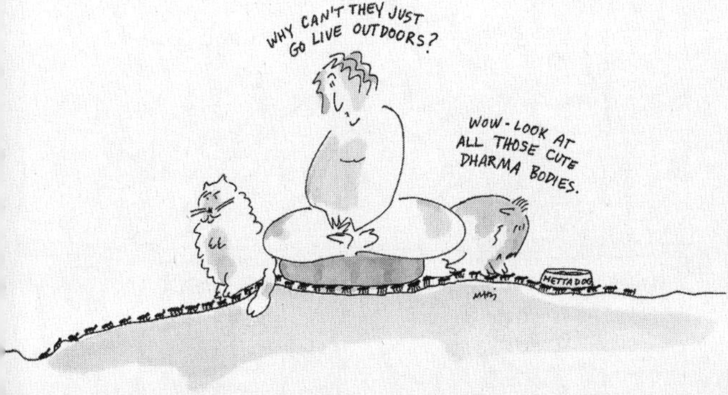
WHY CAN'T THEY JUST GO LIVE OUTDOORS?
WOW - LOOK AT ALL THOSE CUTE DHARMA BODIES.
METTA DOG

Finding compassionate alternatives.

IF BUDDHISM WERE A BREAKFAST CEREAL

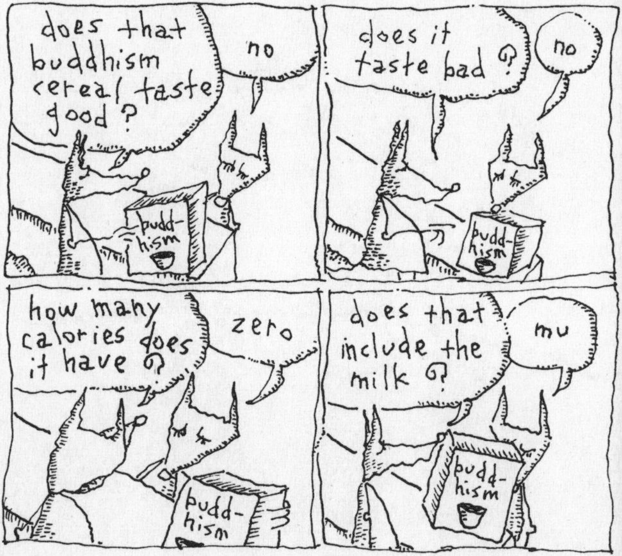
does that buddhism cereal taste good ?
no
budd-hism
does it taste bad ?
no
budd-hism
how many calories does it have ?
zero
budd-hism
does that include the milk ?
mu
budd-hism

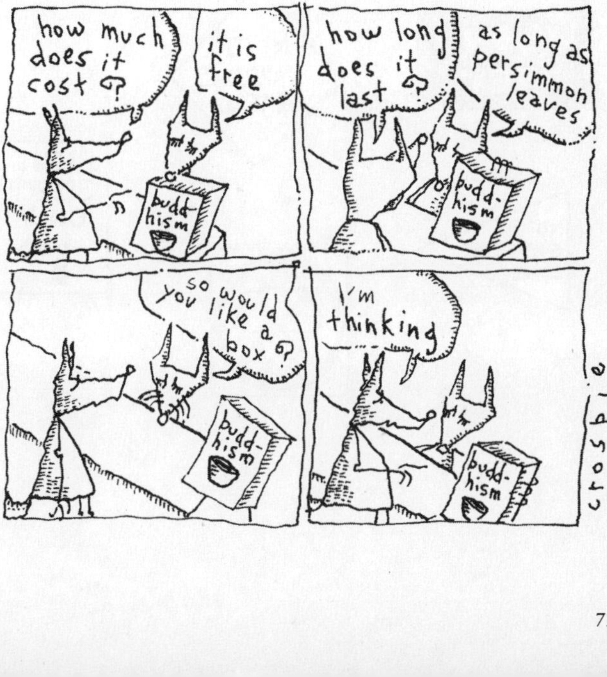
how much does it cost ?
it is free
how long does it last ?
as long as persimmon leaves
so would you like a box ?
I'm thinking
budd-hism
crosbie

WRONG VIEW
MIND NARROWS AHEAD
RIGHT SPEECH ONLY
NO SUFFERING ZONE
Schmidt

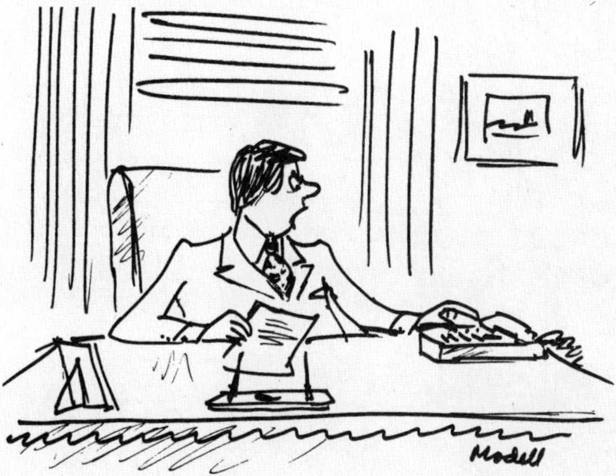
Modell

"Forget the lawyers! You tell him that my roshi will be in touch with his roshi!"

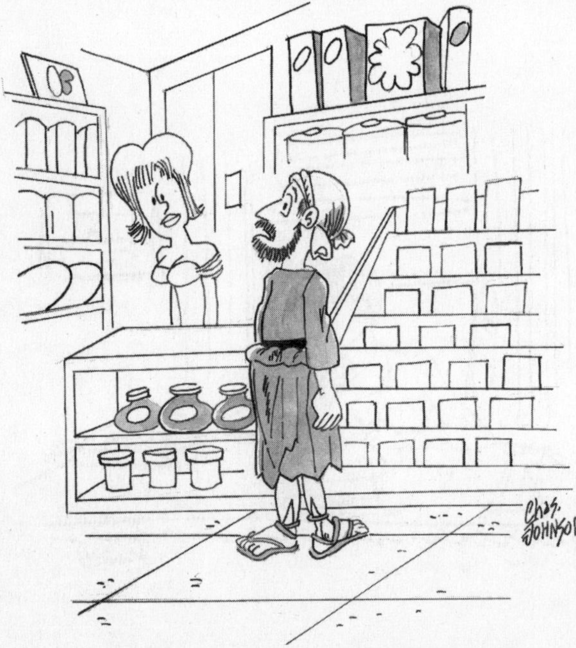
Chas. Johnson

"Do you have cards of congratulations for those who have just attained enlightenment?"

WHEW! AT LAST MY MIND IS CLEAR... SPACIOUS AND ALLOWING... I'M REALLY ALIVE IN THE MOMENT... OR AM I? ACTUALLY I'M THINKING ABOUT NOT THINKING. ABOUT BEING ALIVE... THEREFORE AM I REALLY BEING PRESENT OR JUST PRETENDING TO BE PRESENT WHEN REALLY I... SIGH! INHALE... RIGHT FOOT... EXHALE...
SIGH! HUMANS ARE SO WEIRD!
MAM

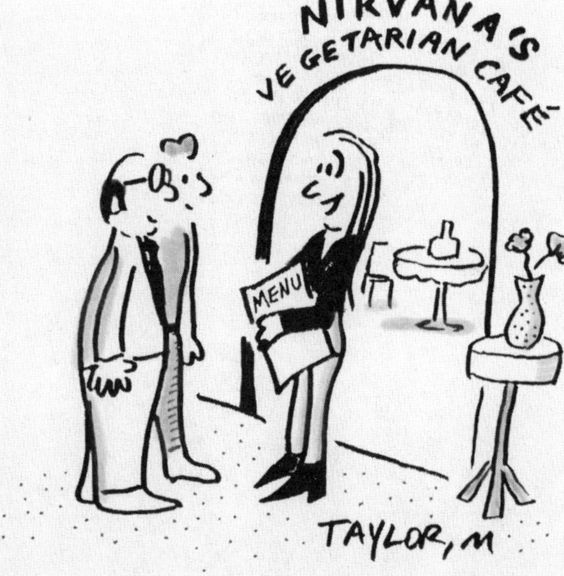
NIRVANA'S
VEGETARIAN CAFÉ
MENU
TAYLOR, M

"Evening, folks—chanting or nonchanting?"

psychedelic person
it must be possible to go beyond the here and now
meditative person
it must be possible to stay in the here and now
normal person
I'll have the nachos special
crosbie

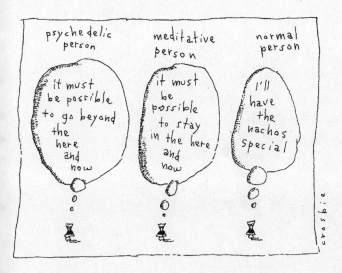

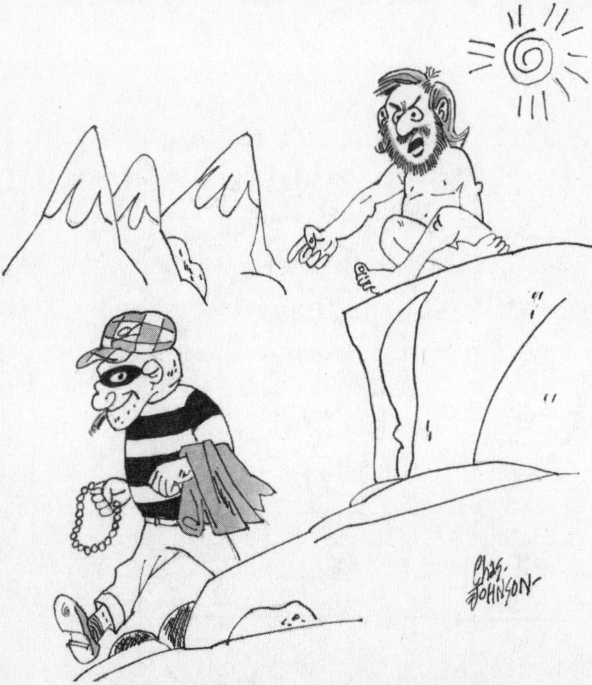
Chas. Johnson

"May you be reborn a thousand times!"

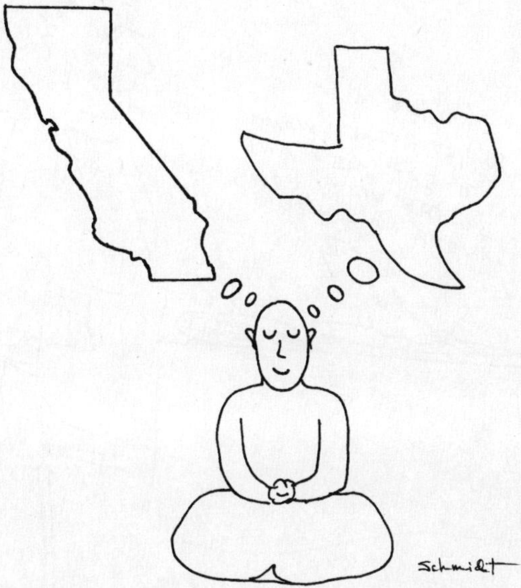
Schmidt

Mental States

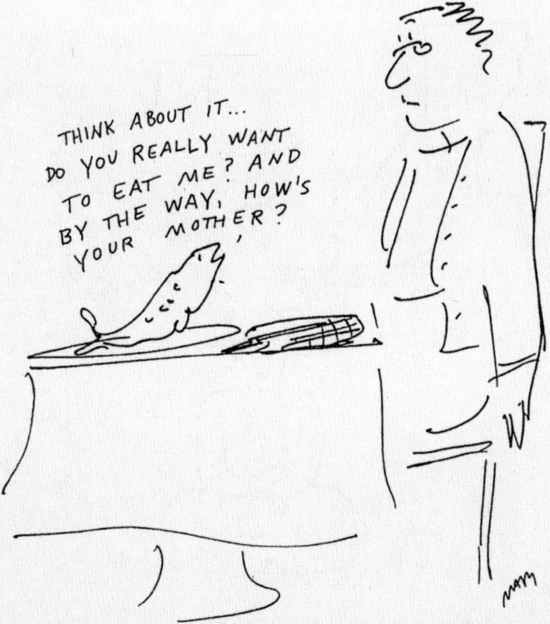
THINK ABOUT IT... DO YOU REALLY WANT TO EAT ME? AND BY THE WAY, HOW'S YOUR MOTHER?

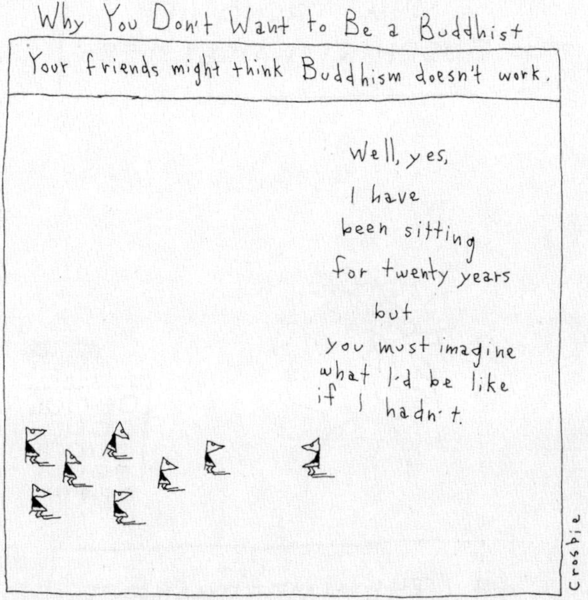
Why You Don't Want to Be a Buddhist
Your friends might think Buddhism doesn't work.
Well, yes, I have been sitting for twenty years but you must imagine what I'd be like if I hadn't.
Crosbie

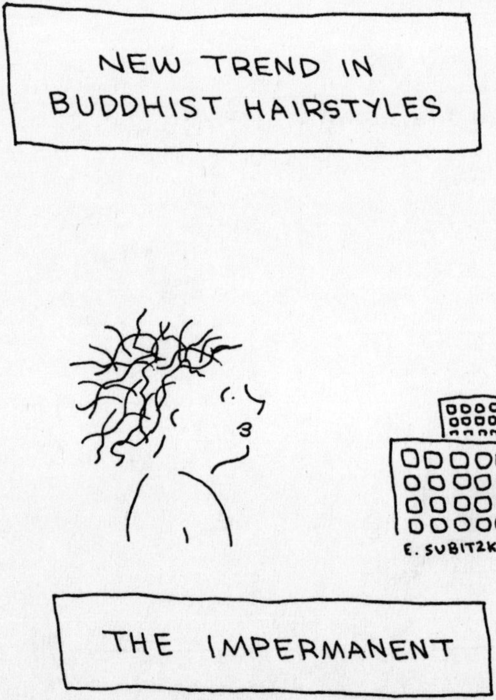
NEW TREND IN BUDDHIST HAIRSTYLES
E. SUBITZKY
THE IMPERMANENT

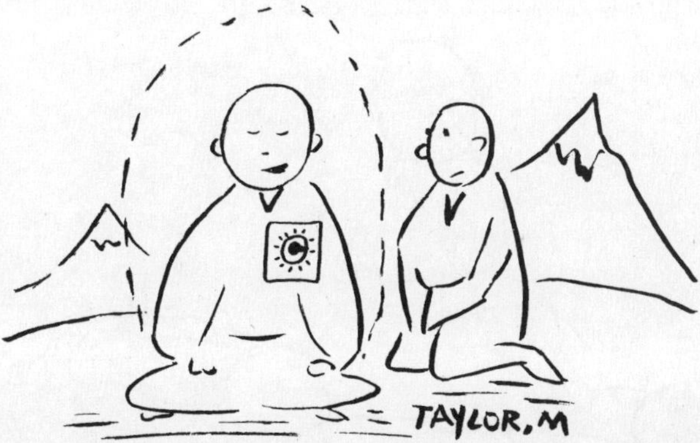
TAYLOR, M

"Would you mind adjusting my thermostat?"

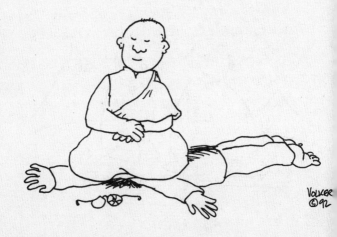

*Beginning students of Vajrayana may have difficulty
visualizing the lama over the top of the head.*

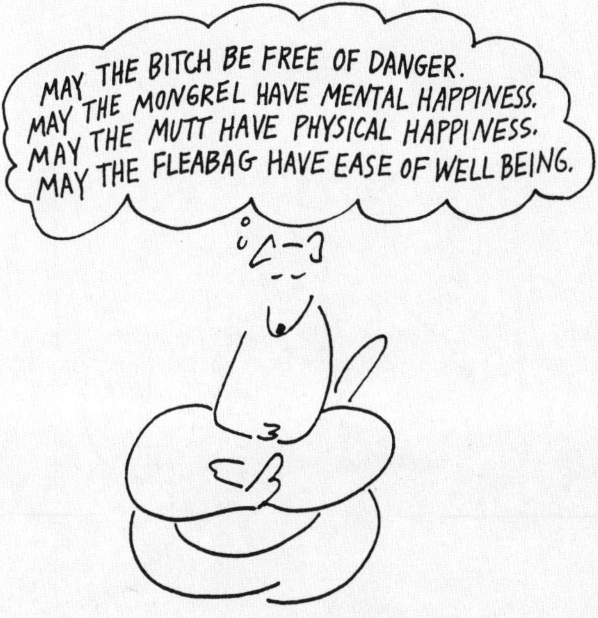
MAY THE BITCH BE FREE OF DANGER.
MAY THE MONGREL HAVE MENTAL HAPPINESS.
MAY THE MUTT HAVE PHYSICAL HAPPINESS.
MAY THE FLEABAG HAVE EASE OF WELL BEING.

Metta in progress.

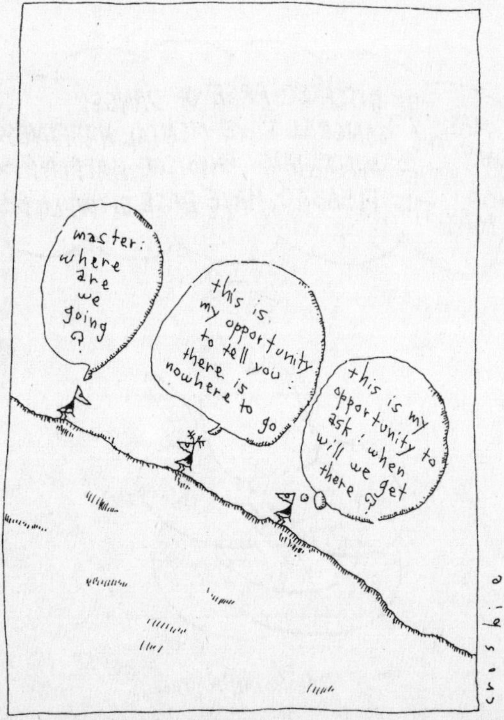
master: where are we going ?
this is my opportunity to tell you: there is nowhere to go
this is my opportunity to ask: when will we get there ?
crosbie

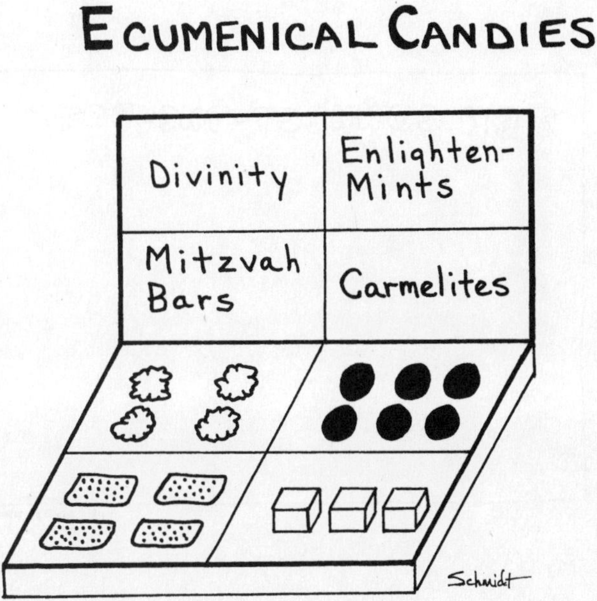
ECUMENICAL CANDIES
Divinity
Enlighten-
Mints
Mitzvah
Bars
Carmelites
Schmidt

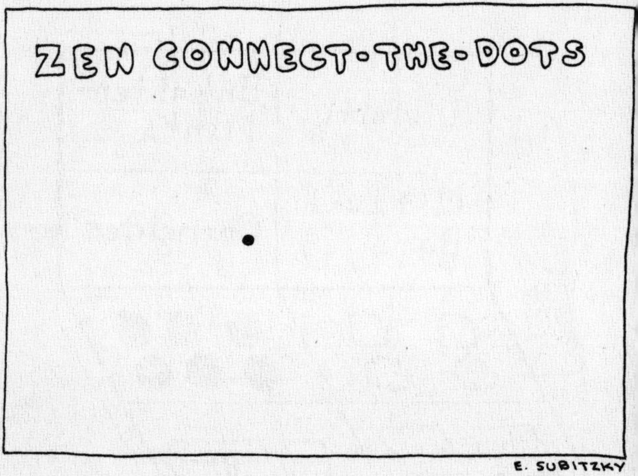
ZEN CONNECT-THE-DOTS
E. SUBITZKY

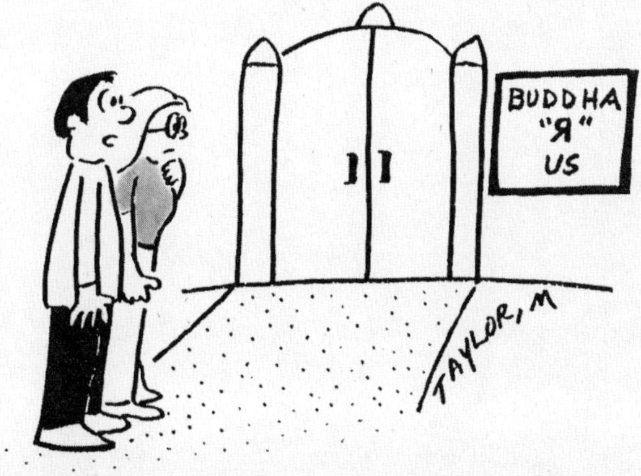
BUDDHA
"Я"
US
TAYLOR, M

"Personally, I liked the old days when we weren't quite so mainstream."

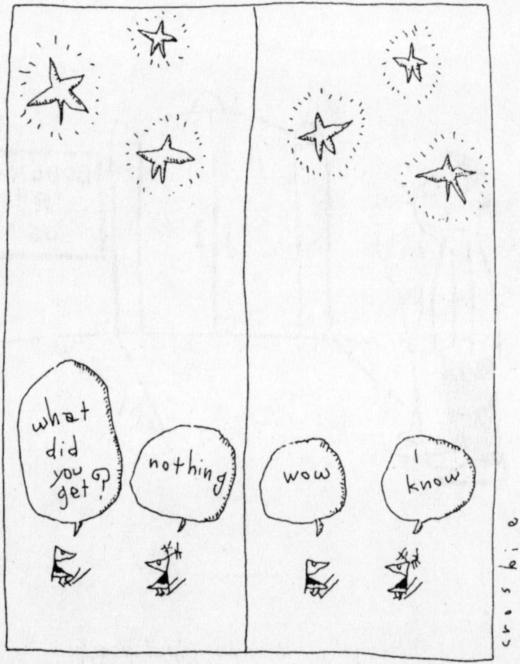
what did you get?
nothing
wow
I know
crosbie

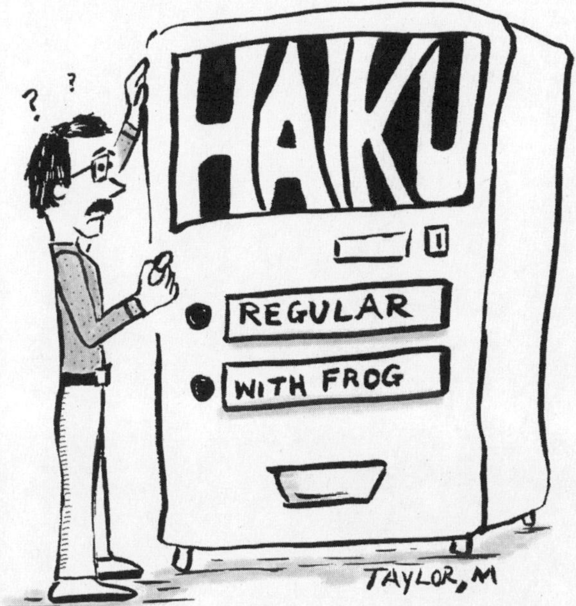
HAIKU
REGULAR
WITH FROG
TAYLOR, M

Aim and sustain your attention.
Cultivate the one-pointed focus of a Border collie.

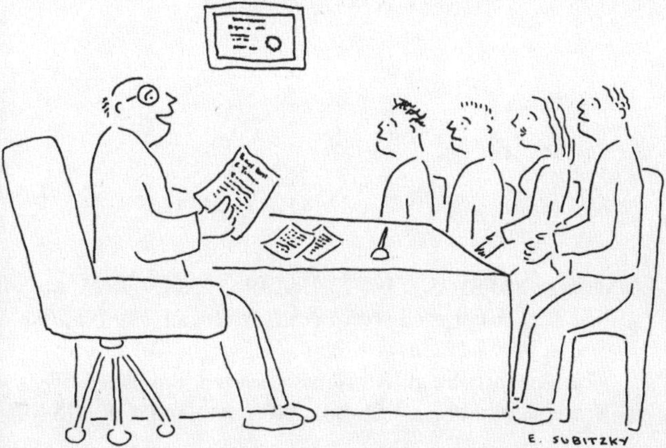
E. SUBITZKY

"And thus, as my last will and testament, I leave all of my belongings to myself in my next life. . . . "

INDEX OF ARTISTS

FRANK OLINSKY 43, 61

LOUISE RAFKIN 24 (Courtesy *Inquiring Mind.*)

SUZIE RASHKIS 10, 35, 44

AMY SCHMIDT 56, 60, 64, 72, 79, 87

AMY SCHMIDT & DAVID BERMAN 12, 36, 45, 53

AMY SCHMIDT & SUSAN THOMPSON 29

HARLEY SCHWADRON 18, 26, 46

DAVID SIPRESS 28, 37, 65

ED SUBITZKY 13, 21, 30, 39, 50, 58, 67, 82, 88, 93

MIKE TAYLOR 15, 31, 40, 51, 59, 68, 76, 83, 89, 91

PAUL VOLKER 17, 84